Walking in the Light of FREEDOM
volume 1

Celebrating African-American History Through
THE SPIRITUAL SONG

By René Boyer-Alexander

HAL•LEONARD® CORPORATION
7777 W. BLUEMOUND RD. P.O. BOX 13819 MILWAUKEE, WI 53213

Copyright © 2002 by HAL LEONARD CORPORATION
International Copyright Secured   All Rights Reserved
No part of this publication may be reproduced in any form or by any means
without the prior written permission of the Publisher.

TABLE OF CONTENTS

Preface	3
Introduction	4
What is Black History Month?	5
Lift Ev'ry Voice and Sing	7
Black History Rondo (Speech Activity)	9
Let's Celebrate Black History	10
A People in Slavery (Choral Speech)	11

Section I: Spirituals – Songs of Sorrow	**15**
Nobody Knows the Trouble I've Seen	16
Sometimes I Feel Like a Motherless Child	17
My Lord, What a Morning	18
There Is a Balm in Gilead	19
I've Been 'Buked	21
Deep River	22

Section II: Spirituals – Songs of Joy	**23**
Ev'ry Time I Feel the Spirit	23
Rock-a My Soul	25
He's Got the Whole World in His Hands	27
Now Let Me Fly	28
Oh, Won't You Sit Down?	30
I Got Shoes!	32
Walk Together, Children	34

Section III: Spirituals – In Search of Freedom	**36**
Mask and Symbol	36
Go Down, Moses	37
Swing Low, Sweet Chariot	38
The Underground Railroad	40
They Were Slaves (Poem)	41
Who Was Harriet Tubman?	42
A Conversation with Harriet Tubman	43
Spirituals Used for the Underground Railroad	46
Steal Away	46
Good News!	47
Get on Board	49
This Train	50
Wade in the Water	51
We Are Climbing Jacob's Ladder	52
Polaris, The Drinking Gourd	53
Follow the Drinkin' Gourd	54
The Life of Frederick Douglass (Choral Speech)	56
Free at Last	60
This Little Light of Mine	61

Section IV: Spirituals – The Dream of Freedom Lives On	**62**
Fisk Jubilee Singers	62
Other Major Composers and Arrangers of the Spiritual Song	62
Conclusion	66
Program Resources	67
The Underground Railroad	67
A Message Through Song	70

PREFACE

The history and spirit of African-American people remain alive in the songs and storytelling that have been passed down through word of mouth for generations. As a result of laws that prohibited literacy among slaves, it was through music that African Americans told of tragedy and triumph, of slavery and the human struggle for freedom.

If one looks and listens carefully, he will find that spiritual songs, plantation songs and folklore, children's songs and games, blues, jazz, gospel and freedom songs clearly reflect how African Americans helped to build and shape America, encouraging it along the path of liberty set out in its founding documents. Moreover, it is through music that African Americans shared their memories of past generations and prepared themselves for the light of a free world that they believed lay ahead.

Today, the fingerprints of African-American music, with its characteristic syncopated rhythms, memorable melodies, attractive harmonic structures and unique performance practices, can be heard in almost every form and style of music: whether in the playful playground chants of children, the passionate evangelism of spirituals and gospel or the sensuous rhythms of blues and jazz.

All Americans share in the music, folktales, and speech activities included in *Walking in the Light of Freedom* and its historical drama continues to touch people struggling for freedom around the world. From the pain and progress of the past, strength and inspiration for the future continue to be drawn.

Enjoy this series, *Walking in the Light of Freedom*. I can assure you that it will be one of your most beloved and cherished possessions.

René Boyer-Alexander

Dr. René Boyer-Alexander is a Professor of Music Education and Director of the Orff-Schulwerk Program at the College-Conservatory of Music at the University of Cincinnati. She is a nationally and internationally recognized author and clinician. Best known for her work in multicultural music education and choral music as they are applied in the urban classroom setting, René's expertise lies in her ability to engage elementary and middle school students in creative and ethnically diverse musical experiences that capture their interest for years to come.

René is a co-author of *Share the Music*, a K-6 basil textbook series published by McGraw-Hill and *Music Fundamentals, Methods, and Materials for the Elementary Classroom Teacher* published by Addison Wesley Longman. Her other publications include *Expressions of Freedom*, an Anthology of African-American spirituals in three volumes published by Hal Leonard Corporation.

INTRODUCTION

The month-long celebration of Black History Month in the United States has gained widespread recognition by educational institutions, religious groups, businesses, government and other organizations. Electronic and print media have been particularly supportive in their efforts to educate American people regarding contributions African Americans have made in the growth and development of our country.

Walking in the Light of Freedom is a resource series designed to enhance the understanding of the history of the African American since their arrival in this country over three hundred years ago. It will focus on a singular, but most important contribution that African Americans have made, and which will also serve as the key to unlocking true understanding of African-American history and culture. That key is **music**.

In order to trace and understand the cultural underpinnings of African Americans, it is necessary to turn to song and storytelling; for it is here that the history and the spirit of the enslaved African remain alive. Through word of mouth and song, the African-American culture managed to pass down from one generation to the next, significant parts of its history – parts that have become integral to the America that we know and love today.

Walking in the Light of Freedom will serve as a major resource guide, to be used throughout the year, in assisting educators, musicians, church attendees, families, and other organizational personnel who wish to learn more about the history of African Americans in this country. The chronological history, contained throughout this series, will serve as a user-friendly way to delve into the inner workings of a culture whose history for hundreds of years had been excluded.

In an effort to allow both young and more mature individuals the opportunity to become involved in learning more about the role African-American music and storytelling have played in the development of our great country, the songs, speech and rhythmic activities, stories and commentaries have been specifically designed to appeal to all levels of understanding. There are many opportunities for a variety of age groups to sing, play melody and rhythmic instruments, play games and participate in creative dramas, all of which will lead to a fun and enjoyable way to learn more about black history.

What Is Black History Month?

Each year, throughout the month of February, Americans stop to recognize the progress, richness and diversity of achievement by African Americans.

Dr. Carter G. Woodson (1875 - 1950), an African American, who was concerned about the lack of mention of African Americans in history books, convinced our nation of the need for this special time.

Dr. Woodson had been born to parents who had been former slaves and consequently witnessed first hand the psychological and physical degradation that many African Americans experienced. Although born in Virginia, he spent his lifetime working in coal mines in Kentucky. He enrolled in high school at age twenty, and two years later was accepted into Harvard, where he later finished his doctorate degree. After graduation, he taught American history. While in the classroom, it became increasingly evident to Dr. Woodson that a vital part of American history was missing. There was little mention in any published materials about the role African Americans had played in the building of their country. He sought to change this by forming a group called the Association for the Study of Negro Life and History. This association published a "Journal of Negro History," to which he regularly contributed. After years of research, that resulted in the publication of sixteen books, Woodson suggested the celebration of Black History Week. He felt that Americans desperately needed this time to learn about and reflect on both the history and teachings of African Americans in an effort to strengthen understanding between the two races.

In 1976 a month-long celebration was implemented. The celebration was broadened to include the birthdays of Abraham Lincoln and Frederick Douglass, the great Negro Abolitionist. February also marked the founding of the National Association for the Advancement of Colored People, NAACP. By the 1920s, the existence of this organization spurred the efforts of African Americans to gather together an identity. By the 1950s, the Civil Rights movement prompted the formation of other organizations to assist the direction that the NAACP had taken in the fight for equal rights.

Today, Carter Godwin Woodson, known as the Father of Black History, would be proud to witness the positive way in which the United States of America has embraced the vision that he espoused so many years ago. Clearly his belief to acknowledge the substantial contributions of African Americans has helped us become stronger and more respectful of one another as a nation.

INTRODUCTION

James Weldon Johnson (1871-1938), a founder of the National Association for the Advancement of Colored People (NAACP), wrote the words to "Lift Ev'ry Voice and Sing" in 1900 to commemorate the birthday of Abraham Lincoln. His brother, J. Rosamond, set the words to music. "Lift Ev'ry Voice and Sing" is known in the black community as the African-American National Anthem and is sung at many predominately black functions. Its text clearly portrays the meaning behind our celebration of this special month. Therefore, it seems only fitting and proper that we should begin here in our musical exploration of Black History Month.

Lift ev'ry voice and sing 'til earth and Heaven ring,
Ring with the harmonies of liberty;
Let our rejoicing rise high as the list'ning skies
Let it resound loud as the rolling sea.
Sing a song full of the faith that the dark past has taught us;
Sing a song full of the hope that the present has brought us.
Facing the rising sun of our new day begun;
Let us march on 'til victory is won.

Stony the road we trod, bitter the chast'ning rod,
Felt in the days when hope unborn had died;
Yet with a steady beat, have not our weary feet
Come to the place for which our fathers sighed?
We have come over a way that with tears has been watered.
We have come, treading our path through the blood of the slaughtered,
Out from the gloomy past, 'til now we stand at last
Where the white gleam of our bright star is cast.

God of our weary years, God of our silent tears,
Thou who hast brought us thus far on the way;
Thou who hast by Thy might, led us into the light,
Keep us forever in the path, we pray.
Lest our feet stray from the places our God, where we met Thee,
Lest our hearts, drunk with the wine of the world, we forget Thee;
Shadowed beneath Thy hand, may we forever stand,
True to our God, true to our native land.

LIFT EV'RY VOICE AND SING

INTRODUCTION

Words by JAMES WELDON JOHNSON
Music by J. ROSAMOND JOHNSON
Arrangement by RENÉ BOYER-ALEXANDER

With spirit (♩. = 80-84)

Lift ev'-ry voice and sing 'til earth and Heav-en ring; ring with the har-mo-nies of lib-er-ty. Let our re-joic-ing rise, high as the lis-t'ning skies; let it re-sound loud as the

Copyright © 2002 by HAL LEONARD CORPORATION
International Copyright Secured All Rights Reserved

7 / Walking in the Light of Freedom – Volume 1

BLACK HISTORY RONDO
(SPEECH ACTIVITY)

Words and Music by
RENÉ BOYER-ALEXANDER

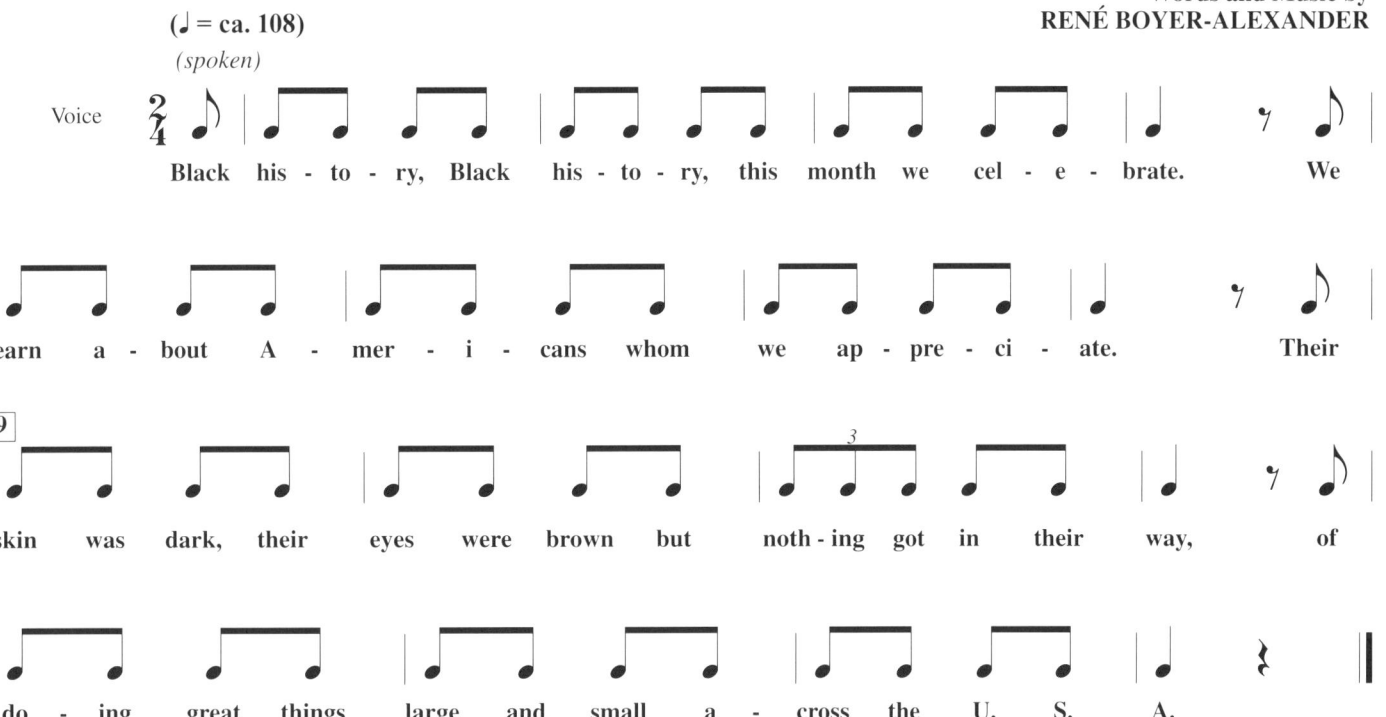

Black his-to-ry, Black his-to-ry, this month we cel-e-brate. We learn a-bout A-mer-i-cans whom we ap-pre-ci-ate. Their skin was dark, their eyes were brown but noth-ing got in their way, of do-ing great things large and small a-cross the U. S. A.

Copyright © 2002 by HAL LEONARD CORPORATION
International Copyright Secured   All Rights Reserved

Use each of the following verses about famous African Americans as alternate sections to be performed as part of the **Black History Rondo**.

Famous African Americans

Harriet Tubman was a slave,
Lots of black folk she did save.
Led them North to liberty,
Only there could they be free!

Frederick Douglass learned to read,
Helped the other slaves in need.
Spoke to them about equal rights,
Equal rights for black and white.

Nat Turner hated being a slave,
He wanted to be free.
He'd speak out loud to anyone,
Including you and me.

Rosa Parks got on a bus,
Refused to sit in back.
She went to jail for doing this
Because her skin was black!

Martin Luther King led a march
To Washington D.C.
Millions joined to help him show
How important it is to be free.

INTRODUCTION

LET'S CELEBRATE BLACK HISTORY

Words and Music by
RENÉ BOYER-ALEXANDER

Black his-to-ry, Black his-to-ry! It's time to cel-e-brate! Black his-to-ry, Black his-to-ry! Come on now, don't be late! Come find out more a-bout his-to-ry; how blacks en-slaved and free, fought for e-qual lib-er-ties so all men could be free!

Copyright © 2002 by HAL LEONARD CORPORATION
International Copyright Secured   All Rights Reserved

10 / Walking in the Light of Freedom – Volume 1

A People in Slavery
(Choral Speech)
By René Boyer-Alexander

Close your eyes and imagine
You're lying down to rest,
After a long day spent with family and friends
You feel secure and blessed.

The night is warm, but peaceful,
The only sounds you hear
Are the gushing ocean waters
And an occasional bird or deer.

When all of a sudden strange men burst in
With guns and weapons in hand,
And lunge upon you so suddenly
And beat you again and again.

They bind you in chains and take you away,
Separating your family and friends.
You try to fight but to no avail,
You simply can't understand.

Your village is left in shambles,
Completely destroyed and burned.
There's terror and fear all in the air,
You're at the "point of no return."

This is what happened in Africa
Just a few centuries ago
Where the people were treated so brutally
Then loaded on ships as cargo.

Conditions on slave ships were horrible,
Packed like sardines in a can.
The slaves were chained in the cargo holds
To be transported to a distant land.

Many of them died from hunger and disease
Many from heart-ache and shame.
They felt like animals in captivity
Though they were hardly to blame.

Some were proud and quickly realized
That slaves they had come to be,
So they jumped overboard, chains and all
To a dignified burial at sea.

Those who arrived in America
Were taken to an auction block
To be examined and sold to freed men
Who saw them as merely livestock.

Their entire bodies were examined,
Their ears and teeth as well
To make sure that they were able and fit
Before they were put up for sale.

They were bought for different prices
Depending on their worth.
Some cost hundreds of dollars,
Others were as cheap as dirt.

They were taken to plantations
To farm, to clean and sew.
They were required to do hard labor
Wherever they would go.

A plantation was a busy place
That grew tobacco and things,
But cotton was the greatest crop
That allowed men to live like kings.

Slave labor was in high demand,
They worked from dawn to dusk.
The shells of cotton blistered their fingers
As did corn with its long green husks.

Days off were simply not heard of
Whether sick or severely in pain.
The slave worked on throughout the day
In burning hot sun or rain.

While field slaves planted and cared for crops,
House slaves had jobs to do.
They did the laundry and cooked the food,
They cared for the children too.

If slaves chose not to do their work
They were whipped and beat real hard.
Their punishment was witnessed by one and all,
Their backs were left ripped and scarred.

Although they were treated badly
They brought both wisdom and skill
To whatever task assigned them
They did with pride and good-will.

Slaves were creative and talented,
They made furniture from handcarved wood.
They were weavers and potters and even iron workers,
They sang whenever they could.

The slaves had been given American names,
African languages had been banned.
They were not allowed to read or write
Neither woman, child, nor man.

They'd lost all things they had known
Their culture, their language and more.
They'd lost their families but their freedom
Was something they had to restore.

They had to search for their freedom,
They had to find a way
To leave the shackles and chains behind,
They prayed to God everyday.

Outwardly they remained obedient
They did as they were told,
But deep within they had the strength
To cleave to a greater goal.

Quakers and many others helped them
To escape to liberty.
These people were called abolitionists,
They believed that slaves should be free.

They helped with the Underground Railroad,
A hidden means of escape
Which led slaves North to freedom
Away from cruelty and hate.

The railroad had a conductor,
It had its depot too,
But more than that it had passengers
Who were slaves being transported through.

The conductor stopped at stations
While hidden, slaves would eat and rest.
They endured harsh weather along their journey,
Freedom was put to a test.

Some slaves were caught and hung on sight
Many made it through,
While others stayed at home to wait
For their chance at freedom too.

The railroad kept on running
For about thirty years or so
Until Abraham Lincoln released the slaves
And all were set free to go.

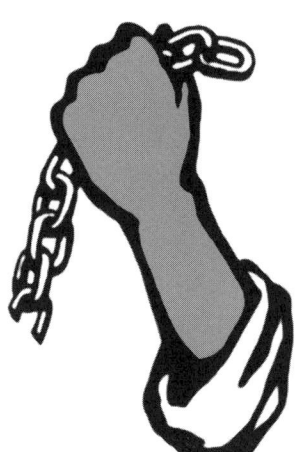

They set out walking away by foot
Not a single penny in hand
To find a place that they could live
In dignity like other men.

Some traveled North, some traveled South
Some traveled East and West
Until they came to a place called home,
A place they could finally rest.

Today there are those who remember
But many Americans do not
The price that was paid for freedom,
Something that should not be forgot.

Suggestion for performance:

- Select either individuals or small groups to recite the verses in sequence.
- Discuss the meaning of the text and how vocal flexibility can be used to express each verse.
- Each individual or group should explore and find the best expressive qualities in choral speech for the verse(s) assigned.
- A slide show that uses pictures or images that enhance each of the verses being performed is recommended.

SPIRITUALS – SONGS OF SORROW

Introduction: The Birth of the African-American Spiritual

After Africans were enslaved and brought to America, they were sold and taken to plantations to help grow crops, cook, clean and care for children. The majority had been separated from family and friends and denied the customs that gave true meaning to their lives. They were not allowed to speak their language and their names were changed.

Shackled with helplessness and despair, African slaves found a recourse for survival. They created the spiritual song. They used the songs to affirm their humanity, build their self-esteem and to give them hope and courage to endure their hardships.

The texts of the spirituals were usually biblical stories that told about people who overcame great odds, bits and pieces of prayers, and sermons. The stories provided role models for all who believed that, like the biblical characters, they too might one day overcome their captivity and again be free. Many spiritual songs contain numerous references to the Israelites in Egypt – Moses, Ezekial, Abraham, Elijah, Jacob and others; while references to harps, crowns, robes and wings are referred to continually in the Book of Revelations.

The slaves often painted pictures through their songs that told of the negative and degrading conditions they were experiencing. The simple and repetitive texts cry out messages of sadness and despair that leaves both performer and listener emotionally caught up in the inescapable plight of the slave poet. "Nobody Knows the Trouble I've Seen," "Sometimes I Feel Like a Motherless Child," "My Lord, What a Morning," "There Is a Balm In Gilead," "I've Been 'Buked" and "Deep River" represent some of the clearest examples of the deep felt emotions that slaves possessed. Each of these spirituals should be performed slowly with sensitivity and understanding.

THERE IS A BALM IN GILEAD

Traditional Spiritual
Arrangement by
RENÉ BOYER-ALEXANDER

SECTION I: SPIRITUALS — SONGS OF SORROW

There is a balm in Gi-le-ad to make the wound-ed

whole. There is a balm in

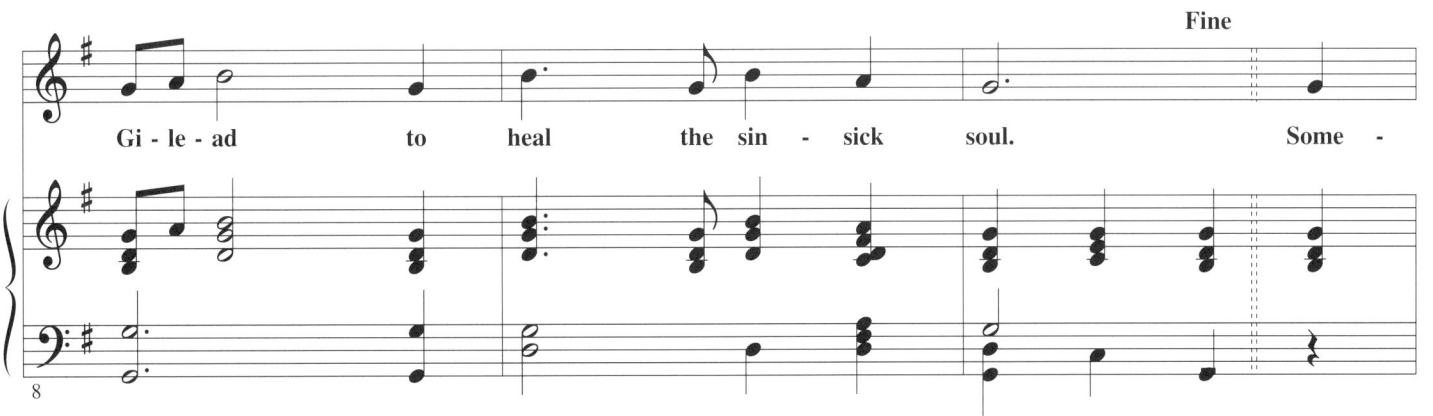

Gi-le-ad to heal the sin-sick soul. Some-

Copyright © 2002 by HAL LEONARD CORPORATION
International Copyright Secured   All Rights Reserved

19 / Walking in the Light of Freedom – Volume 1

SECTION I: SPIRITUALS — SONGS OF SORROW

times I feel dis-cour-aged and think my life's in vain. And

then the Ho-ly Spir-it re-vives my soul a-gain.

D.C. al Fine

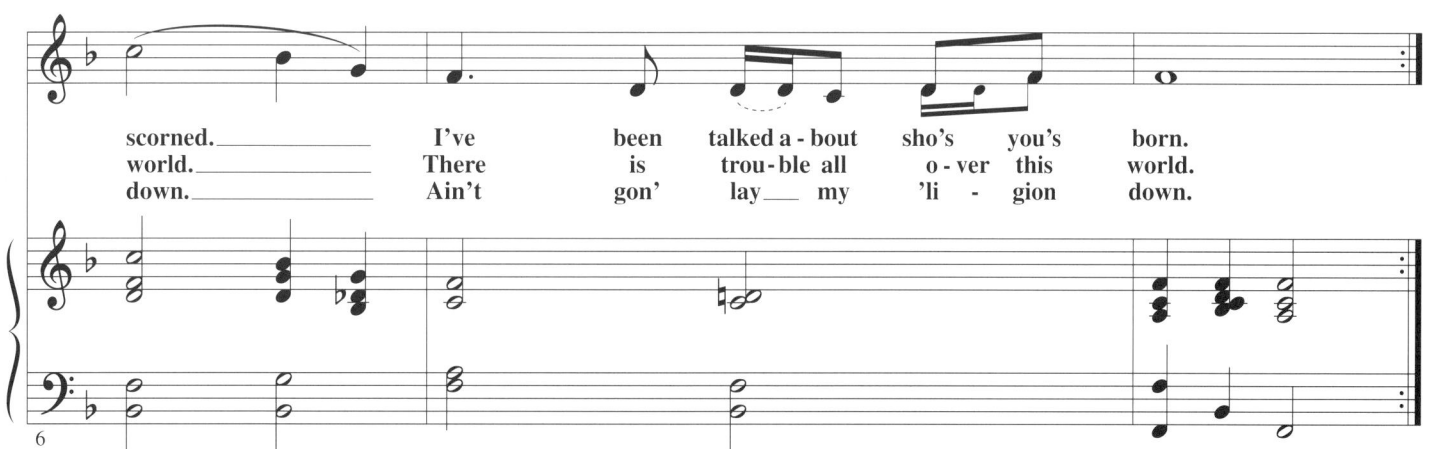

SPIRITUALS — SONGS OF JOY

In addition to songs of sadness that depicted hardship among slaves in bondage, were songs that held the dreams of freedom. These songs were uplifting in spirit. Marked by faster tempos and interesting rhythms, these spirituals provided windows of joy and happiness to men, women and children, who otherwise had limited outlets of expression. "Ev'ry Time I Feel the Spirit," "Rock-a My Soul," "He's Got the Whole World in His Hands," "Now Let Me Fly," "Oh Won't You Sit Down," "I Got Shoes," and "Walk Together Children" represent only seven of the hundreds of spirituals that brought feelings of jubilance to the slave community.

Today these spirituals have become an integral part of our world community. Many are included in textbooks and many have been arranged for use in both secular and sacred choral settings.

EV'RY TIME I FEEL THE SPIRIT

Traditional Spiritual
Arrangement by RENÉ BOYER-ALEXANDER

Copyright © 2002 by HAL LEONARD CORPORATION
International Copyright Secured   All Rights Reserved

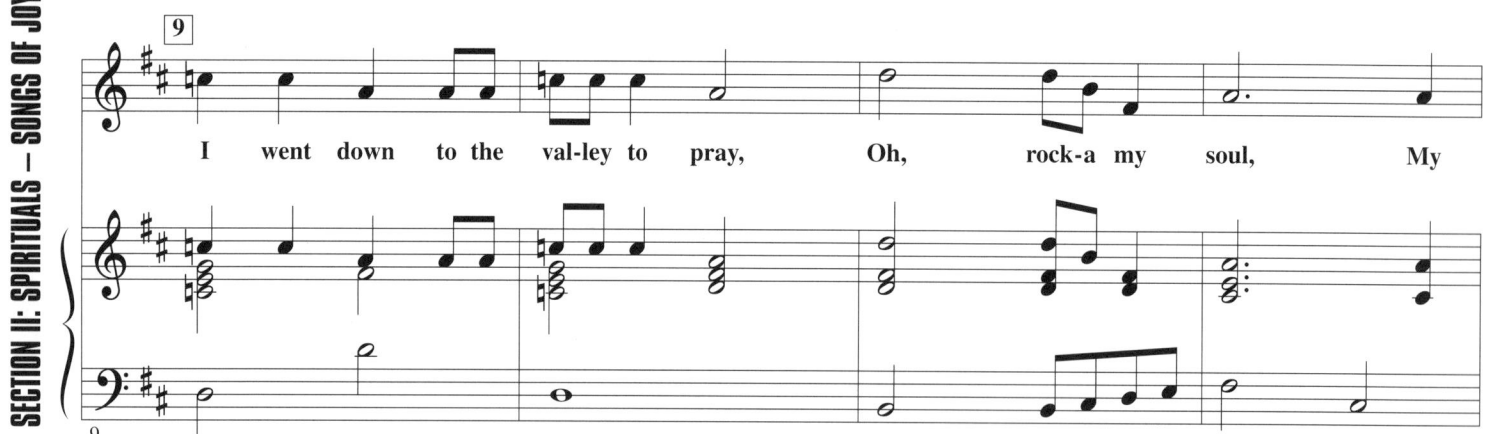

HE'S GOT THE WHOLE WORLD IN HIS HANDS

Traditional Spiritual
Arrangement by
RENÉ BOYER-ALEXANDER

NOW LET ME FLY

Traditional Spiritual
Arrangement by
RENÉ BOYER-ALEXANDER

Copyright © 2002 by HAL LEONARD CORPORATION
International Copyright Secured   All Rights Reserved

OH, WON'T YOU SIT DOWN?

Traditional Spiritual
Arrangement by RENÉ BOYER-ALEXANDER

SECTION II: SPIRITUALS — SONGS OF JOY

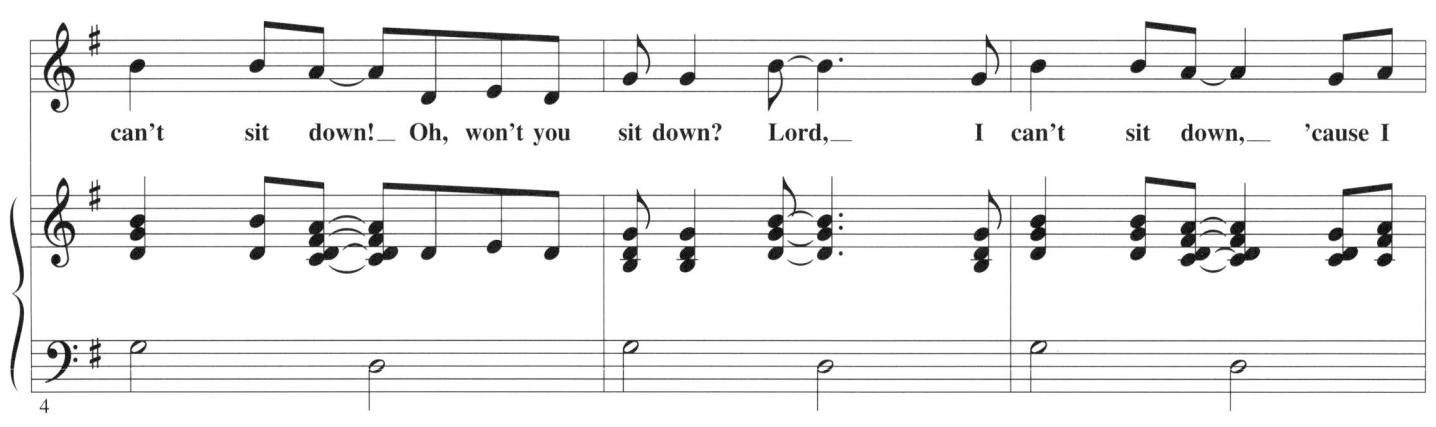
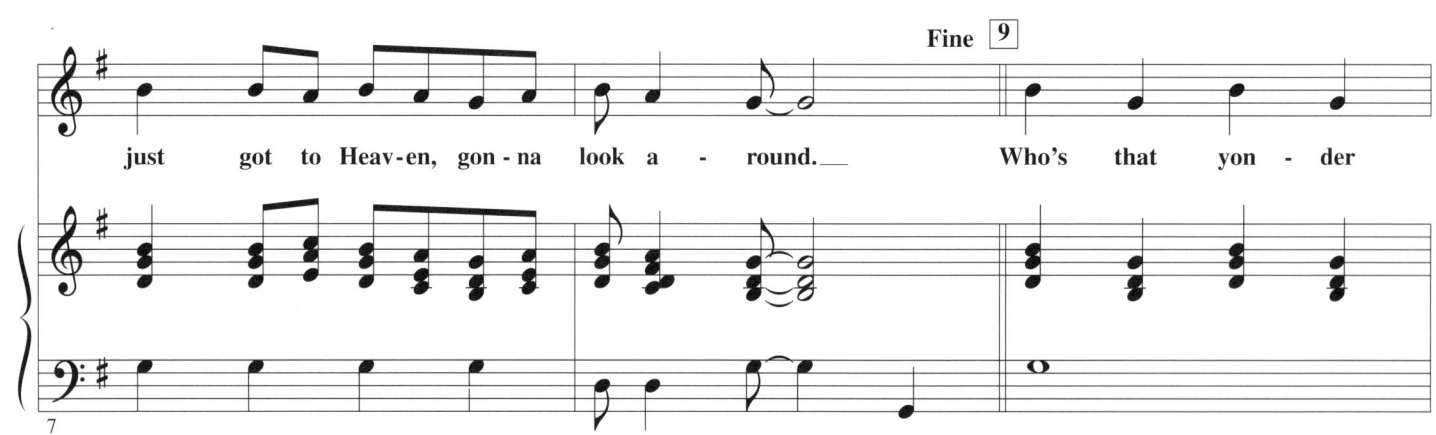

Copyright © 2002 by HAL LEONARD CORPORATION
International Copyright Secured   All Rights Reserved

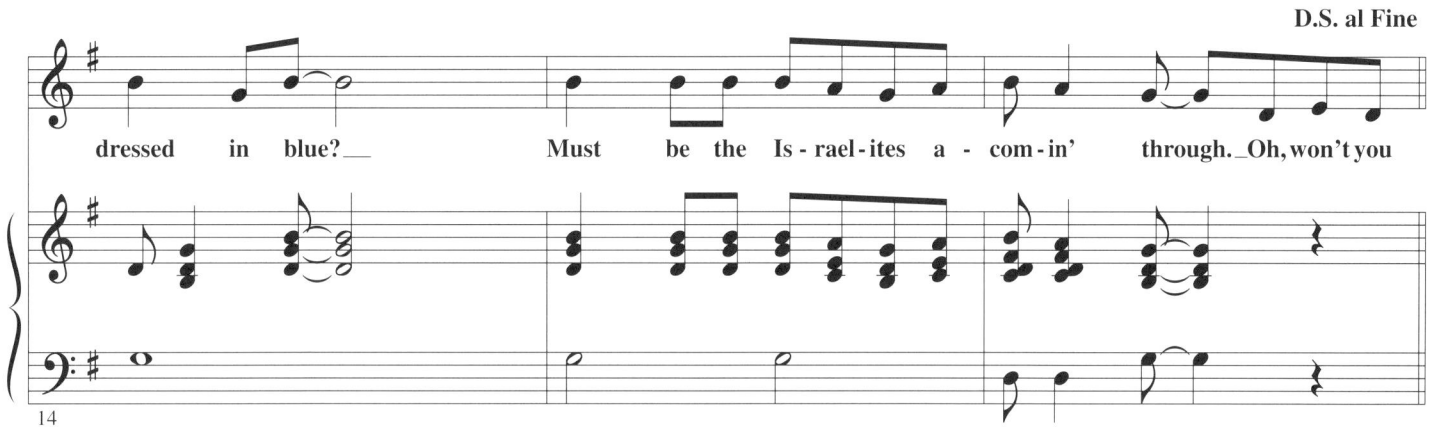

I GOT SHOES!

Traditional Spiritual
Arrangement by
RENÉ BOYER-ALEXANDER

WALK TOGETHER, CHILDREN

Traditional Spiritual
Arrangement by
RENÉ BOYER-ALEXANDER

SPIRITUALS – IN SEARCH OF FREEDOM

Mask and Symbol

Because slaves realized the horrible consequences regarding discussion about escape, they began to use and create songs that contained coded messages that only they could understand. This technique, called *mask and symbol* turned into one of the slaves' most powerful strategies for escape.

It seemed reasonable to the slave community that since the slave owners were placated with the hearing of the beautiful and melodious music that flowed from slave communities, it should be this same music that would unify them as they planned escape. Thus, the slaves began to mask the true meaning of their spiritual songs so that fellow slaves would only understand them.

Two examples of spirituals containing *mask and symbol* are translated below. However, there are numerous others, some of which have been included in the pages that follow.

The Spiritual Text	"Mask and Symbol"
Go Down Moses	*Go down Harriet Tubman*
Way down in Egypt land	*Way down in the southern part of the United States*
Tell old, Pharaoh	*Tell the slave owners and overseers*
To let my people go!	*To let the slaves go.*
Swing Low, Sweet Chariot	*The "chariot" refers to the Underground Railroad*
Coming for to carry me home	*Carry me home to freedom*
Swing Low Sweet Chariot	*The Underground Railroad*
Coming for to carry me home.	*Carry me home to freedom.*

Mention of terms like the *Jordan River* and *heaven* became direct allegorical references to the Ohio River and Canada. In addition, references made to trains, chariots, boats and marching by foot were recognized by the slave community as vehicles that allowed them to escape to freedom by way of one of the most clever escape systems known to man, the *Underground Railroad*.

"Steal Away," "Good News," "Get on Board" and "This Train" were all used to mask escapes. "Steal Away" for example, although sacred in nature, in one respect is heard as evidence of the slaves' resignation to be content by meditating and praying (stealing away) to Jesus, who would pacify them through their hard times. Also, on the surface, it expresses a realization that some slaves felt: there could be no earthly reward to justify their horrible plight, and that they hoped their prayers would hasten them to heavenly peace. On the other hand, slaves who were discontent with their misery, and intent on running away, used "Steal Away" to transmit coded messages to one another. *Steal* (run away), to *Jesus* (the Northern part of the Unites States or Canada); *thunder* and *trumpet* (some sound such as the ringing of a bell, a field holler, calling the hogs, or whatever was used in the midst of the unsuspecting slavemasters or overseers, would signal the escaped runaway slave).

SWING LOW, SWEET CHARIOT

Traditional Spiritual
Arrangement by
RENÉ BOYER-ALEXANDER

38 / Walking in the Light of Freedom – Volume 1

what did I see?__ Com-in' for to car-ry me home? A band_of an - gels

com-in' af - ter me.__ Com-in' for to car-ry me home.

D.S. al Fine

Swing

39 / Walking in the Light of Freedom – Volume 1

The Underground Railroad

The Underground Railroad was an intricate network of people and places designed to help slaves escape to freedom in the North. It involved the secret transporting of fugitive slaves from safe house to safe house, steadily moving until freedom was secured. The people who organized and helped the escaped slaves included prominent citizens, Quakers, and ex-slaves who believed that slavery was wrong.

The transportation of slaves obviously had to be done in secrecy. The transport worked much like a railroad. Once a slave escaped and managed to make contact with sympathizers, he or she became a part of the Underground Railroad and would hopefully be transported to freedom. Similar to an actual railroad, the act of transporting the escaped slaves incorporated all the terms used during a railroad journey.

- The routes from safe house to safe house (houses where fugitives were kept) were called "lines."

- Stopping places were called "stations."

- Those who aided fugitive slaves were called "conductors."

- In order to keep terms as clear as possible, the fugitive slaves were known as "packages" or "freight."

The average distance needed to be covered by a newly escaped slave, in order to arrive at a station was approximately 15 miles. At the stations, the weary slaves were given food, a place to rest, and a change of clothing.

The Underground Railroad stretched for thousands of miles, from Kentucky and Virginia across Ohio and Indiana. Northward it stretched from Maryland, across Pennsylvania and into New York and New England.

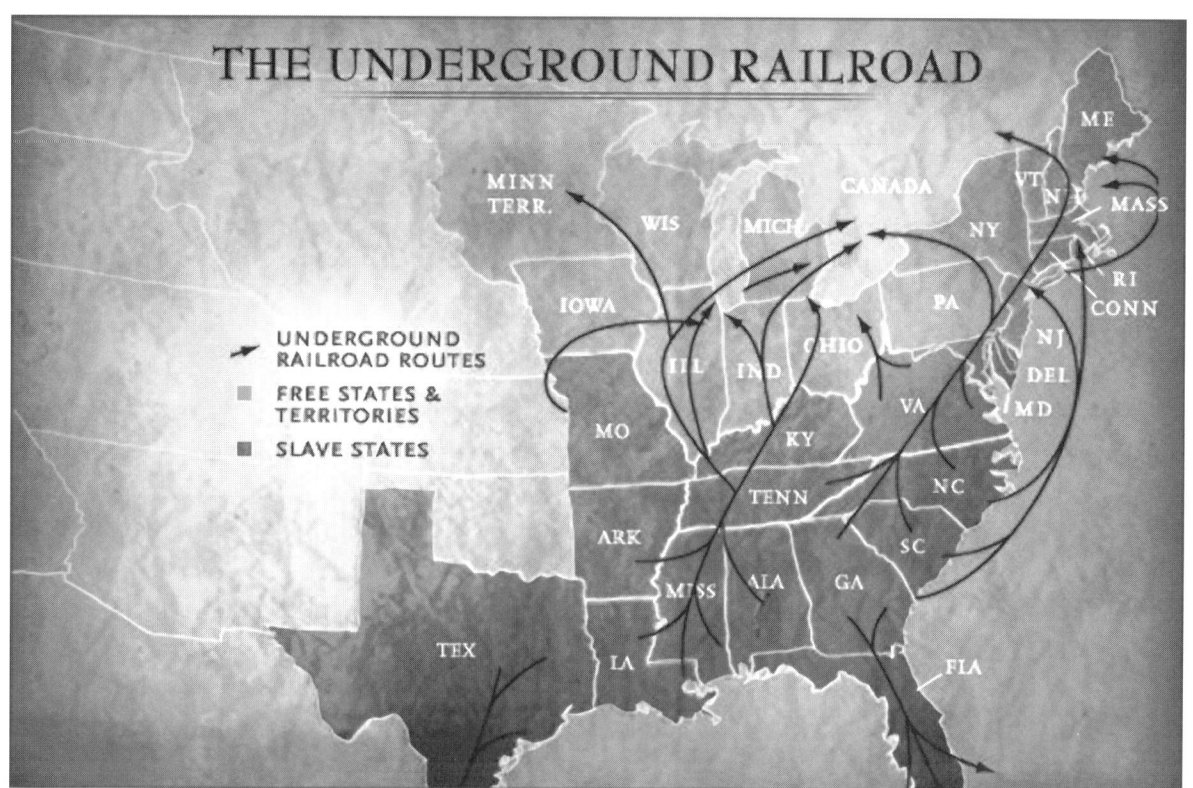

They Were Slaves
Ruth Rene White

And they came up out of the South,
With no destination specific,
And they silenced their singing mouths,
While walking northward, triumphant!

For freedom did they yearn,
With minds, both thoughtful and bright.
They stole away on Freedom's Train
Under soft ebony cover of night.

Who Was Harriet Tubman?

Harriet Tubman played a major role in freeing slaves. After freeing herself from slavery, Harriet returned to Maryland to rescue other members of her family. In all, she is believed to have led over 300 persons successfully to freedom in the North. Today, she is not only remembered as one of the most successful "conductors" of the Underground Railroad, but is also called the "Moses of her people."

Many of the spirituals that are sung today were used by Harriet Tubman and others to help slaves escape to freedom. For example, she used "Go Down, Moses" to alert slaves who wanted to escape. The song forewarned them that a trustworthy guide was approaching to collect them and guide them to freedom. She also used "Wade in the Water" to throw bloodhounds off the scent. Nat Turner, a major leader of slave revolts and uprisings, used "Steal Away" to call his conspirators together. "Follow the Drinkin' Gourd" (the drinking gourd was the Big Dipper in the sky) was a musical and poetic map of one line in the network of the Underground Railroad.

In addition to Harriet Tubman, celebrated conductors of the Underground Railroad included James Fairfield, a white abolitionist who traveled into the Deep South and rescued enslaved African Americans by posing as a slave trader.

African American John Parker of Ripley, Ohio frequently ventured to Kentucky and Virginia to help transport hundreds of runaways across the Ohio River by boat.

William Still, Robert Purvis, David Ruggles and others organized and stationed vigilance committees throughout the North. Vigilance committees were designed to offer whatever assistance needed to help escaped slaves reach freedom.

A Conversation With Harriet Tubman
(A Choral Dialogue)
By René Boyer-Alexander

Question: Harriet, Harriet
               What'cha gonna do?

Harriet: Lead those slaves,
               Right on through!
               Gonna lead 'em in the night;
               Gonna lead 'em in the day;
               Gonna lead those slaves
               Towards freedom's way.

               Song: "This Train" or "Swing Low, Sweet Chariot"

Question: Harriet, Harriet
               How're you gonna go?

Harriet: Gonna take that railroad
               To and fro,
               Gonna stop at the station
               And load my train,
               Gonna travel with my cargo
               Through the snow and rain.

               Song: "Get on Board"

Question: Harriet, Harriet
               But you're nothin' but a slave.
               If you get caught
               You'll be in your grave.

Harriet: No grave's so deep
               To stop me now.
               I'll free as many slaves
               As the Lord'll allow.

               I'll follow that Dipper
               With that great big star.
               It will lead me North,
               Who knows how far.

               Song: "Follow the Drinkin' Gourd"

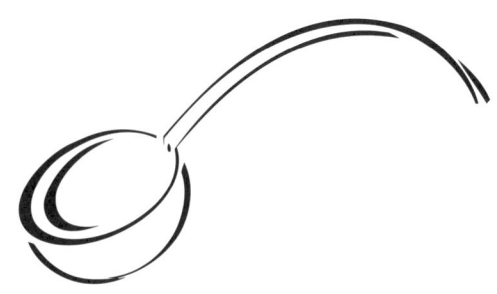

Question:	Harriet, Harriet As I hear you speak, Do you have the strength? You look so weak.
Harriet:	I have the strength. I have the power. I have what it takes In my weakest hour. Believe it or not I am not alone, The Lord is with me And this makes me strong.
	Song: "Rock-a My Soul"
Question:	Harriet, Harriet You're all right, You remind me of Moses And the Israelites. He led his people Through the big Red Sea, He led them on to Victory!
	Song: "Go Down, Moses"
Harriet:	Yes indeed, I'll agree, I've worked for freedom And for victory. But this I know As long as I stand, Freedom will be present All across this land!
	Song: "Now Let Me Fly"
Question:	Harriet, Harriet Aren't you scared? The slaves you lead Are not prepared,

To endure the rain,
The ice and snow.
If something goes wrong
Where will you go?

Harriet: We'll all go to heaven,
We'll all be free,
We'll all experience our liberty.
Doesn't matter what happens
I know it's true,
That the Lord above
Will carry us through.

Songs: "Walk Together, Children"
"This Little Light of Mine"

GOOD NEWS!

Traditional Spiritual
Arrangement by
RENÉ BOYER-ALEXANDER

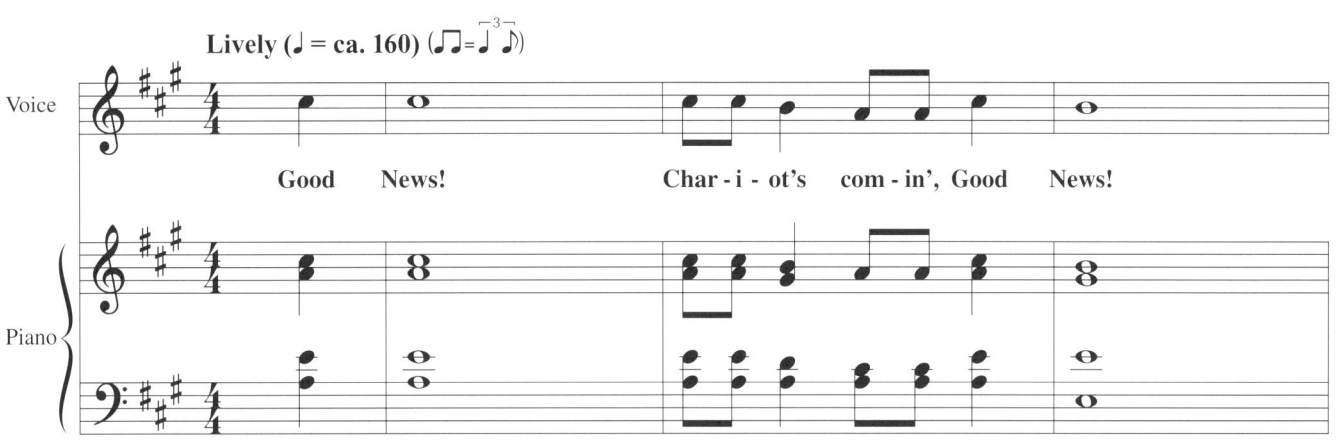

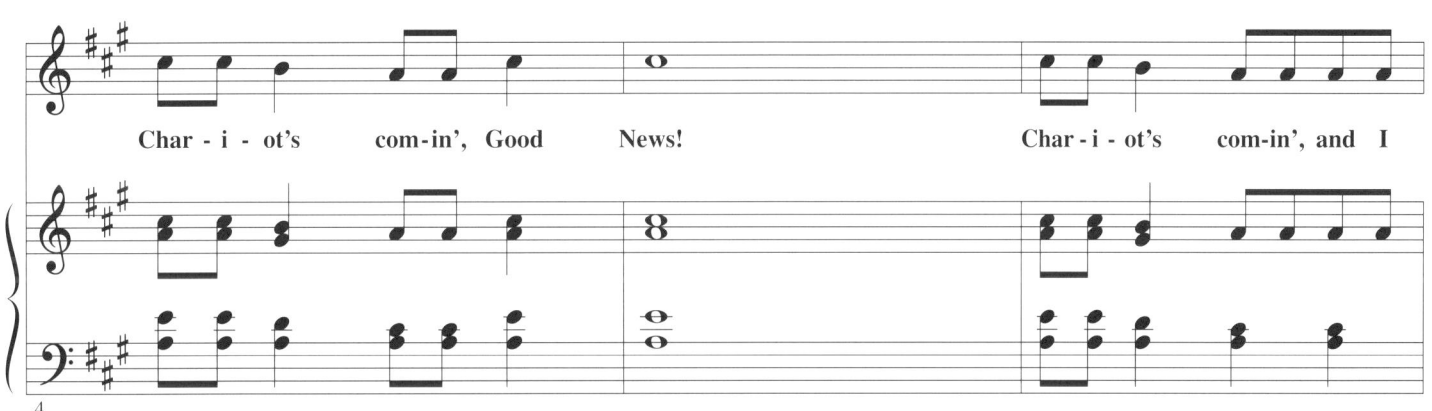

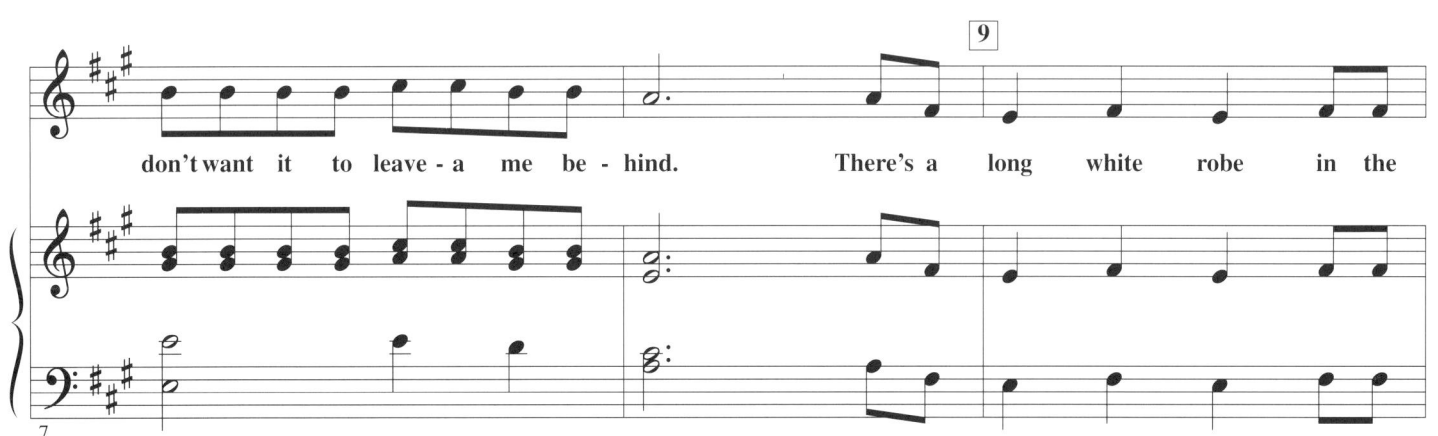

THIS TRAIN

Traditional Spiritual
Arrangement by
RENÉ BOYER-ALEXANDER

WADE IN THE WATER

Traditional Spiritual
Arrangement by
RENÉ BOYER-ALEXANDER

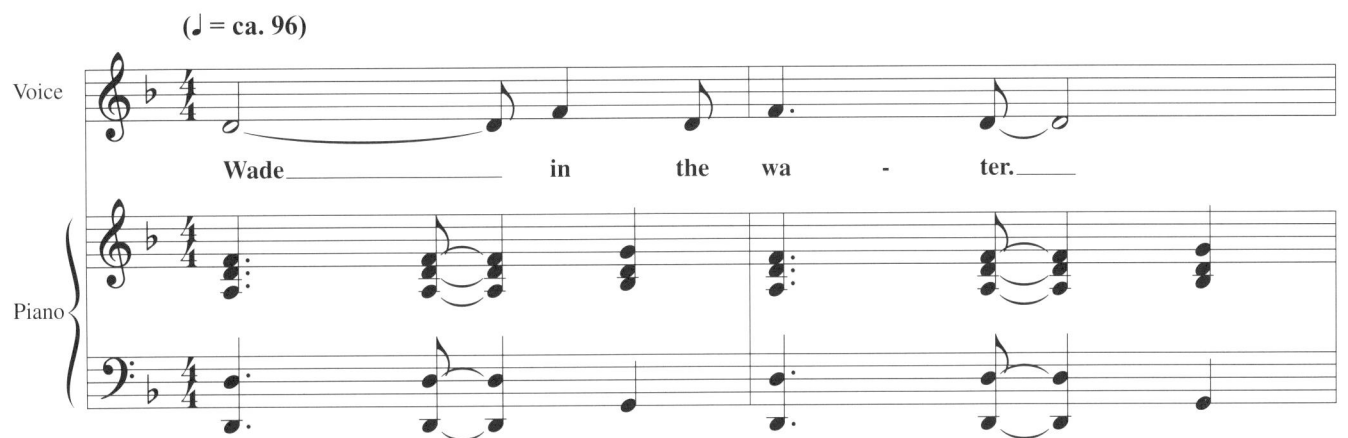

WE ARE CLIMBING JACOB'S LADDER

**Traditional Spiritual
Arrangement by
RENÉ BOYER-ALEXANDER**

Copyright © 2002 by HAL LEONARD CORPORATION
International Copyright Secured   All Rights Reserved

"Climbing up" was terribly important to the slave; he felt he had been kept down for too long. The slave viewed the story of Jacob as a point of departure. The slave's determination to rise from his low estate, like Jacob, and to progress up the material and spiritual ladder, "rung by rung" was critical. Jacob's experience was chosen because it was perhaps one of the most dramatic and impressive of the Biblical stories.

Polaris, The Drinking Gourd

In order to reduce the number of escaping slaves, owners kept slaves illiterate and totally ignorant of geography. Owners even went so far as to try to keep slaves from learning how to tell directions. Slaves, however, knew perfectly well that freedom lay in the North. They knew how to locate North. They used the North Star, or as it is properly named, *Polaris* to guide them. Polaris lies almost directly north in the sky.

In 1831, members of the Underground Railroad began to send travelers into the South to secretly teach slaves specific routes they could navigate using Polaris. By the beginning of the Civil War in 1861, about 500 people a year were traveling in the South teaching slaves of well established escape routes. Many scholars estimate that 60,000 to 100,000 slaves successfully fled to freedom.

Polaris became a symbol of freedom to slaves as well as a guide star. As soon as they were old enough to understand, slave children were taught to locate Polaris by using the stars of the Big Dipper. The Big Dipper, in turn began to be referred to as the "Drinking Gourd," because it resembled the shape of major cooking and eating utensils used in their native country, Africa.

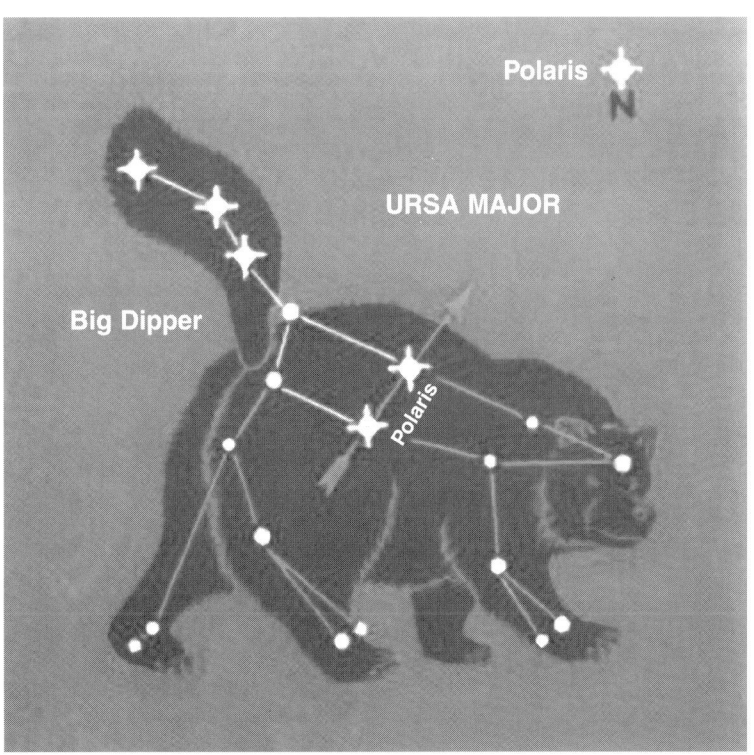

FOLLOW THE DRINKIN' GOURD

Traditional Spiritual
Arrangement by
RENÉ BOYER-ALEXANDER

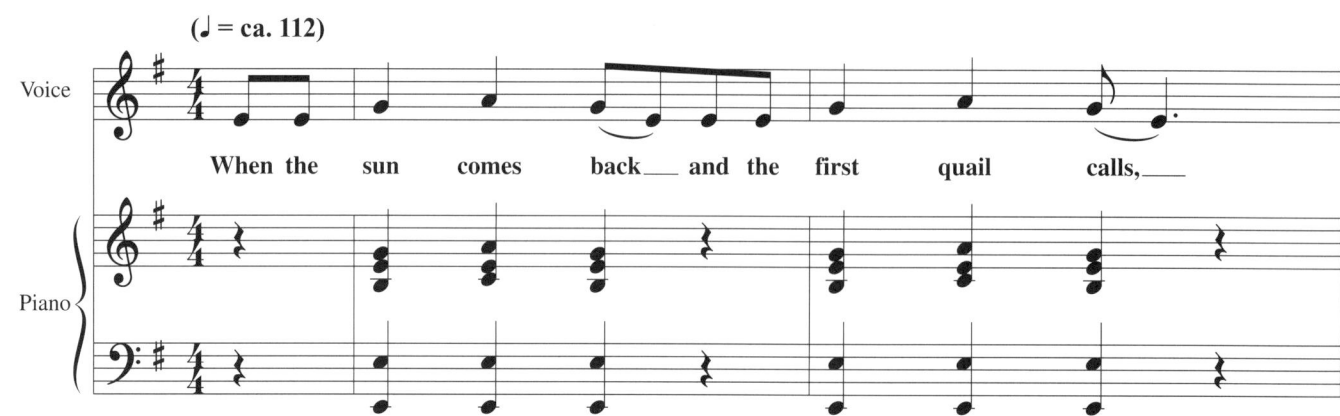

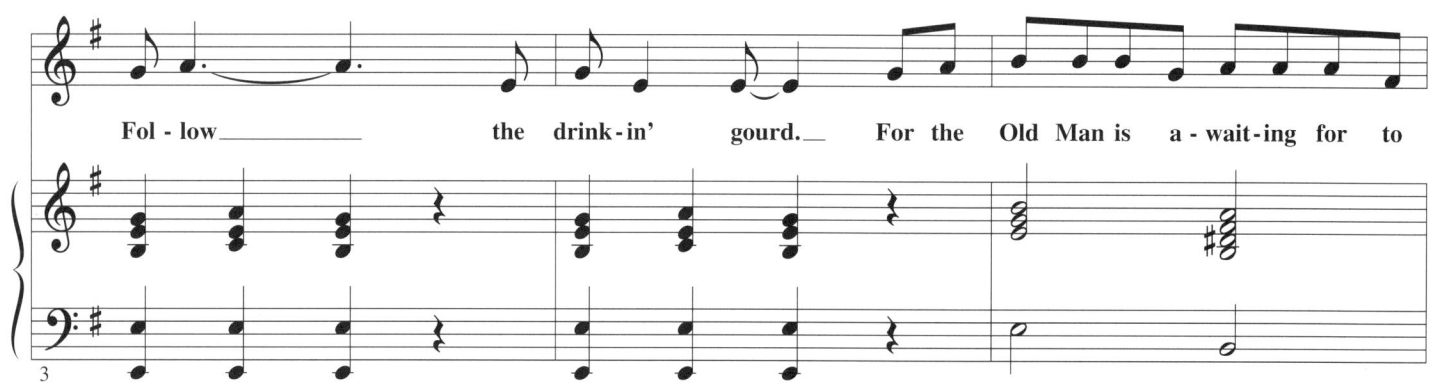

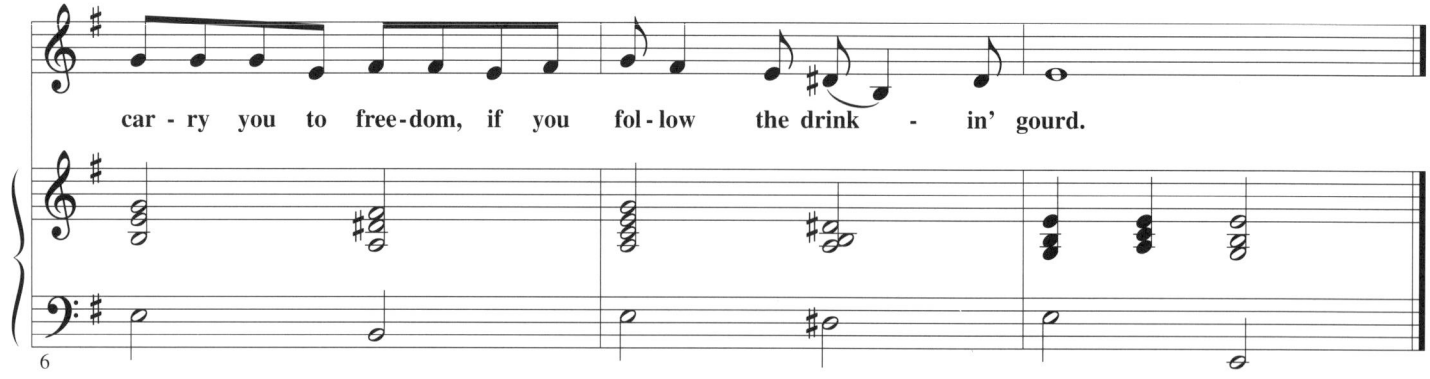

(Follow the Drinkin' Gourd, cont.)

"Follow the Drinkin' Gourd" is a coded song that gives the route for an escape from Alabama to Mississippi. Of all the routes out of the Deep South, this is the only one for which the details survive. The route instructions were given to slaves by an old man named Peg Leg Joe. Working as an itinerant carpenter, he spent winters in the South, moving from plantation to plantation, teaching slaves about a successful escape route.

When the Sun comes back
And the first quail calls (1)
Follow the Drinkin' Gourd.
For the old man (2) is a-waiting
For to carry you to freedom
If you follow the Drinkin' Gourd.

The Riverbank (3) makes a very good road.
The dead trees will show you the way.
Left foot, peg foot, traveling on (4)
Follow the Drinkin' Gourd.

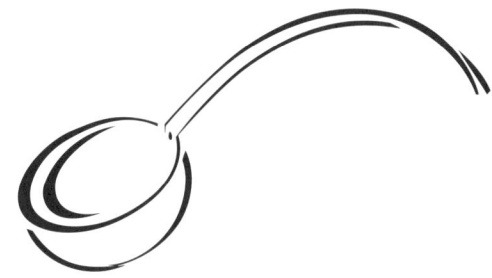

The river ends between two hills
Follow the Drinkin' Gourd.
There's another river on the other side (5)
Follow the Drinkin' Gourd.

When the great big river meets the little river (6)
Follow the Drinkin' Gourd.
For the old man is a-waiting
For to carry you to freedom
If you follow the Drinkin' Gourd.

(1) This refers to the changing of the seasons. On the winter solstice, the Sun rises in the southeast. In the months after the December solstice, the Sun rises more northerly and ascends higher in the sky. Quail, migrating from the north, winter in the south.
(2) Peg Leg Joe
(3) Tombigbee River, leading northward from the Gulf of Mexico toward Tennessee.
(4) Dead trees were used as markers with charcoal and mud drawings of a peg leg and a foot.
(5) Tennesse River, which flows northward across Tennessee and Kentucky.
(6) This is where the Tennessee River and the Ohio River merge (over 800 miles north of Mobile). It was here that Underground guides would meet fugitive slaves on the northern bank and transport them to safer regions. A slave who left a plantation in southern Alabama or Mississipi in the winter would arrive at the Ohio River about a year later. The best time to cross the Ohio River was when one could simply walk across the ice.

Frederick Douglass

In spite of it being a serious crime to learn to read and write during slavery times, many slaves sought every opportunity to learn this skill. Frederick Douglass was one of them. In his book, *Narrative of the Life of Frederick Douglass*, published in 1845, he recounts the harsh life on pre-Civil War plantations on which he lived and worked before escaping to New York. He describes the senseless cruelty of slave masters and the debased lives of slaves. The Choral Speech that follows, retells the story of this great African American man.

The Life of Frederick Douglass

(Choral Speech)
By René Boyer-Alexander

He was born in 1817
As I've been told;
And his name was Frederick Bailey,
Now the story unfolds.

As a slave he had no future,
He only had a dream.
In many ways he was the same
As Martin Luther King.

Frederick learned so very quickly,
What it meant to be,
A slave in life and never have
Your equal liberty.

It meant sleeping on the floor
Because you had no bed,
It meant saying "yes" to master,
No matter what was said.

Frederick watched the older slaves
Who worked from dawn to dusk.
He saw them whipped, he saw them beat,
Deep down he felt disgust.

"Why are we slaves?" he asked
The old folk far and near,
"Is it something that we've done?
You seem to be in fear?"

"Hush!" his Grandma told him,
As she sternly looked about.
"You're a slave, that's a fact,
A boy who has been bought."

"We don't question things in life
That we cannot control.
You'll learn a lot about these things
As you, my boy, grow old."

At eight years old, young Frederick
Was sent to Baltimore.
While he was there his life improved
In ways unthought before.

His master's wife Sophia
Took on the awesome chore
Of teaching Fred to read and write
She felt he should know more.

But then one day, his books were gone.
His lessons promptly ended;
Because his Master Auld found out,
And he was quite offended.

"What have you done?" He asked his wife,
"Your actions are absurd!
A slave must never read or write!
Not a single word!"

Frederick's 16th year was horrid,
He moved from Baltimore.
He ended up in places
He'd never seen before.

He was forced to do hard labor
Was whipped, until one May
He turned upon his master and said,
"No more of that today!"

He beat his Master Covey,
Knocked him to the ground.
Fought him hard until he sent
His master homeward bound.

To hit your master was a crime,
Punishable by death
But Covey took no action,
He let the matter rest.

One day when Fred was older,
He joined a team of five,
They planned escape to freedom
A dream they kept alive.

A younger slave who joined them,
Grew more and more afraid,
Until he told of Frederick's plan,
Destroying plans they made.

Slave owners in the city
Had no proof of a plot,
But all agreed that Fred must leave
Or else he would be shot.

He then returned to Baltimore,
The home of Master Auld
He hired on at a shipyard,
He earned money and saved it all.

It was here he met more black men,
Some were slaves and some free,
He joined a club renown to all,
As the Mutual Society.

Once a week they'd gather,
To read and write and talk
Until at last he figured out
It was time to "walk."

One day in 1838
Fred climbed aboard a train
And in that nervous moment
He became a runaway slave.

He arrived in New York City
He had no food to eat,
He had no job, had no home,
He had no place to sleep.

He met a man named Ruggles,
An Abolitionist,
Who hid him in a safe house,
Where he could eat and rest.

His name was changed to Douglass
To ward off anyone,
Who hunted for a black man
Who'd taken off and run.

As Frederick Douglas settled in,
He wrote his thoughts all down.
He told stories of slavery,
Of Africans chained and bound.

He published a book in '45,
It was a great success.
It told the story of his life
A cause for much unrest.

He fled to England to escape
The pain he left behind.
And there he found his freedom
Among men, both good and kind.

In England he raised money
To buy his liberty.
In eighteen hundred forty-seven,
Frederick was now free.

FREE AT LAST

Traditional Spiritual
Arrangement by
RENÉ BOYER-ALEXANDER

SPIRITUALS – THE DREAM OF FREEDOM LIVES ON

The Fisk Jubilee Singers

From the mid-1800s, most black colleges formed groups of jubilee singers and/or vocal quartets to sing spirituals. These groups toured the nation and represented the institution outside the local community. One of the earliest and most prestigious of these groups was the Fisk Jubilee Singers from Fisk University in Nashville, Tennessee. Under the direction of George L. White, this group set out to raise money for the struggling university founded in 1866. Over the decade, they had toured most of the northern states, had performed at the White House, toured England and much of Europe and had played for Queen Victoria.

The group had been given its name by their director. In <u>Old Testament</u> history, each fiftieth Pentecost was followed by a "year of jubilee"–a year in which Hebrew law required that all slaves be set free. Organized in 1871, in the dark shadow of slavery, the "Jubilee Singers" seemed a most appropriate name. Most of the students at Fisk had been former slaves.

Other Major Composers and Arrangers of the Spiritual Song

The Fisk Jubilee Singers led the way for others to preserve and cherish these most unique songs that had evolved from slavery. Some of the major preservers of this art form have been:

1. **George White** (1838-1835)
   - choral director who organized the Fisk Jubilee Singers.

2. **Roland Hayes** (1887-1977)
   - famous African-American lyric tenor who was the first to promote the singing of solo spirituals on the concert stage.

3. **Marion Anderson** (1902-1993)
   - internationally famous contralto who was a popular force in popularizing the spirituals and in maintaining the respect and dignity of the songs. She was the first African American to sing at the Metropolitan Opera in New York.

4. **Paul Robeson** (1898-1976)
   - one of the most accomplished of the spiritual singers. His physical appearance, voice range and control, and tremendous emotional color and variety made him one of the most sought after singers of spirituals throughout the world.

5. **Harry Thacker Burleigh** (1866-1949)
   - did more than anyone else in preparing the spiritual for use by concert singers, both individuals and groups. His arrangements are still popular today.

6. **Anton Dvorak** (1841-1904)
    - Czech composer who stressed the importance of African-American music in America. He challenged American composers to use the wealth of material in this treasury of folk music. He is best known for the black spiritual and folk song melodies he used in his *New World Symphony*.

7. **Samuel Coleridge-Taylor** (1875-1912)
    - born in England of African and British parentage, he had a great deal to do toward building the prestige of the African-American spiritual in Europe. Inspired by the Fisk Jubilee Singers, he used "Nobody Knows the Trouble I See" in his *Song of Hiawatha*. As a pianist, his repertoire included "Three Negro Melodies" symphonically arranged from "Set of Twenty-four," a new work composed by Harry Burleigh.

8. **Nathaniel Dett** (1882-1943)
    - educated at Oberlin College, he was a teacher, choirmaster, arranger and composer. He arranged many spirituals in his *Religious Folk Songs of the Negro* and in *The Dett Collection of Negro Spirituals*. He was a firm believer in the religious significance and power of the spirituals.

9. **Edward Boatner** (1898-1981)
    - taught in Texas and settled in New York. He conducted a studio, directed church and community choirs and arranged Negro spirituals that were sung by concert artists.

10. **William Levi Dawson** (1899-1990)
    -director of the Tuskegee Choir, he never used the word spiritual to refer to this music. In his estimation, "spiritual" was too limiting for the songs. He believed that the folk songs would last for a thousand years and would be one of the things for which American blacks would be remembered. He is the composer of the *Negro Folk Symphony* and arranger of some of the finest concert spirituals for choirs ever written.

11. **Hall Johnson** (1888-1970)
    - important in the history of the spiritual because of his remarkable success in directing choirs, arranging songs, and teaching others the arts of directing and arranging as well as genuine flavors of Black music. He was the director of the choirs that sang in *Green Pastures*, which opened on Broadway in 1930, *Way Down South*, and *Cabin in the Sky*.

12. **Rosamund Johnson** (1873-1954)
    - brother of James Weldon Johnson. He organized *The Book of American Negro Spirituals* (1925) and *The Second Book of American Negro Spirituals* (1926). These spirituals serve as standard collections. In 1940, these two books were brought together as *The Books of American Negro Spirituals*.

13. **Frederick J. Work** (1880-1942), **John Wesley Work** (1871-1925) and **John W. Work** (1901-1968)
    -These three musicians were members of a team who carried on the very great tradition in spirituals at Fisk University.

14. **William Grant Still** (1895-1978)
    - recognized as a skilled and creative craftsman. Still used Negro folk melodies as a base for many of his works. He published *Twelve Negro Spirituals, Three Rhythmic Spirituals for Voice and Keyboard Instruments* and *The Devotion of a People*, containing thirteen spirituals. He is best known for this Afro-American Symphony (1931), his *Symphony in G minor* (1937) which he named "Song of a New Race." His Works for Band (1945) include "From the Delta," part work song, part spiritual, part dance. His *Four Indigenous Portraits for String Quartet and Flute* has a section called "North American Negro," an original theme in the style of a spiritual.

15. **Jester Hairston** (1901-2000)
    - remarkable director and arranger of spirituals. His work in later years centered around directing choirs in motion pictures. He published two books of spirituals and has arranged fifty spirituals for individual presentation through sheet music. He did the choral music for the film *Lilies of the Field*. His arrangement of "Amen" was the one used by Sidney Portier in winning the Academy Award for best actor. He was a major actor and character in the television show, *Amen*.

16. **Dorothy Maynor** (1910-1996)
    - one of the leading concert artists who toured widely throughout the world, appearing with major symphony orchestras and giving recitals where she included spirituals. She founded the Harlem School of the Arts in New York.

17. **Mahalia Jackson** (1911-1972)
    -African-American concert artist. Although a world-famous gospel singer, Mahalia Jackson contributed a great deal to the popularity and general appreciation of the African-American spiritual. She specialized in singing spirituals such as "Standing in the Need of Prayer" and "Sometimes I Feel Like a Motherless Child."

18. **Margaret Bonds** (1913-1972)
    - African-American composer, pianist and teacher. In 1932, she won the Wanamaker prize in composition for the song "Sea Ghost". She was the first black soloist with the Chicago Symphony Orchestra. Later in her career, she made arrangements of spirituals for Leontyne Price. These arrangements now belong to the classical repertoire of most black singers.

19. **Leontyne Price** (1927-___)
    - concert artist who could sing any spiritual superbly well. Within her rearrange of spirituals her favorite arranges are Margaret Bonds, Harry T. Burleigh, Hall Johnson, Edward Boatner and Florence Price.

The end of the 20th century and beginning of the 21st century introduced to the world a plethora of new and more powerful arrangers and performers who have taken the spiritual to even greater heights.

One of the more captivating of arrangements is that of "Lift Ev'ry Voice and Sing." Roland Carter, Professor of Choral Music at Memphis State University arranged "Lift Ev'ry Voice and Sing," adding to it a more powerful rhythmic base, a contemporary harmonic structure and an expanded vocal range. It is clearly one of the most powerful pieces created in the 20th century.

Some other major arrangers and performers include:

20. **Moses Hogan**
    - internationally renown pianist, conductor, and arranger. His contemporary choral settings of spirituals and other works have been praised by choral directors and audiences all over the world.

21. **Brazil Dennard**
    - choral director, composer and arranger of African American spirituals.

22. **Kathleen Battle**
    - lyric soprano who is a world acclaimed singer. Included in her European based classical repertoire is a host of spiritual arrangements for solo voice.

23. **Willis C. Patterson**
    - Professor Emeritus of Voice and Associate Dean at the University of Michigan, Patterson is a composer and arranger of spirituals. He also served as President of the National Association of Negro Musicians and Executive Secretary of the National Black Music Caucus. He continues to promote the study and performance of the spiritual art form.

24. **Jessye Norman**
    - dramatic soprano who is one of the world's most sought-after artists. She made her operatic debut in 1969 but continues to perpetuate the African-American spiritual as a living art form, which is of great importance to world music.

25. **Sylvia Olden Lee** (Retired from the Curtis Institute of Music)
    - the foremost authority in the style of the African-American spiritual. She has served as coach to such great names as William Warfield, Jesseye Norman and Kathleen Battle.

CONCLUSION

The month-long celebration of Black History has given our global community an opportunity to take a more indepth look at the contributions of the African American. Clearly, the creation of the African-American spiritual is without question one of the greatest of these contributions.

The spiritual sang primarily of the life and aspirations of slaves. It was deeply realistic and, without paradox, full of mask and symbol. It was the expression of a folk community that had sung its way through generations, some which span to millennium.

Within the texts, lay a deep sorrow (occasioned by the contemplation of the human condition), the deep understanding of the human struggle (not just of the slaves' struggle), and the deep joy of knowing that faith could overcome any bad human condition.

Today, the spiritual song continues to appeal to people throughout the world. They are proof of the indestructible goodness and power to survive and conquer, not only in African Americans but people everywhere. They give us a promise of victory we know we can trust.

We, as Americans, were reminded of the need for such trust when two planes flew into New York City's World Trade Center on September 11, 2001, killing thousands of innocent people.

The greatness of the spiritual song remains alive as we are reminded of the second verse of "I've Been 'Buked", *"Dere is troubles all over this worl'."*

Herein is the spiritual's prime greatness. They offer faith, hope and truth for all mankind. They continue to offer triumph and the ideals of freedom and justice.

Wherever spirituals touch the world's people, who perpetually need to rebelieve in freedom and justice and man's individual greatness, the world's people sing!

PROGRAM RESOURCES

The Underground Railroad
By René Boyer-Alexander

Most children would say it's a choo-choo train,
With billowing puffs of smoke;
That makes its way across the land
From L.A. to Roanoke.

Its conductor wears a blue-striped cap
Its porters handle bags
As they leave the depot far behind
Waving a bright yellow caution flag.

The whistle screams out for all to hear
As the train rolls down the track
It crosses the countryside mile after mile
As its wheels sound clickity-clack.

This is the picture most children paint
When mention is made of railroads
But I'm here to tell you of a different view
But first we must unravel a code.

The slaves in the South were hopelessly lost
They suffered in captivity
So they created, what most thought, an ingenious scheme
For those who wished to be free.

Songs were used to warn them
That it was safe to go
Songs whose words would tell a tale
That only the slaves would know.

(Perform "This Train")
This train is bound for glory, this train.
This train is bound for glory, this train.
This train is bound for glory,
If you ride it you must be holy,
This train is bound for glory, this train.

(Perform "Get On Board")
So get on board, little children
Get on board, little children
Get on board, little children
There's room for many-a more.

The spiritual song spoke of "glory."
To slaves this meant a free land.
The spiritual songs invited all to board
There was room for every man.

When hearing the songs, people gathered
With no food or clothes in hand
They were guided by a conductor
To escape to freedom's land.

They traveled throughout the darkness
They slept throughout the day
They were part of an Underground Railroad
That led towards freedom's way.

They let the North Star guide them
Found at the tip of the drinking gourd
Which was outlined in the sky so clearly
By their great and powerful Lord.

(Perform "Follow the Drinkin' Gourd")
Follow the drinkin' gourd,
Follow the drinkin' gourd
For the old man is awaiting
For to carry you to freedom if you
Follow the drinkin' gourd.

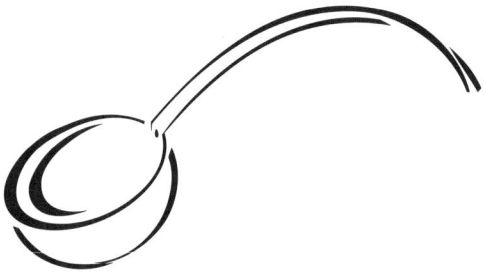

The conductor led the passengers
Across the countryside.
They'd stop at a depot or safe house
Where they would rest and hide.

Some slaves would climb a ladder
Which led to a hiding place.
Beneath a barn or shed or room
From the danger, they did face.

(Perform "Jacob's Ladder")
We are climbing Jacob's Ladder
We are climbing Jacob's Ladder
We are climbing Jacob's Ladder
Soldiers of the cross.

When the sounds of dogs came nearer
You could hear a quiet hum.
To wade in the water, all God's children
In the water, they would overcome.

(Perform "Wade in the Water")
Wade in the water.
Wade in the water, children.
Wade in the water.
God's a-gonna trouble the water.

The water erased all signs of them
Their smells and scents were gone.
The power of song, saved their souls
But chilled them to their bones.

Soon the conductor would arrive
Cargo safe in hand
In a place where all freed slaves could live.
Like any other man.

End with the audience joining in to sing "Free at Last" and "This Little Light of Mine."

A Message In Song
By René Boyer-Alexander

Narrator 1:
Good afternoon. African-American History Month is observed throughout the month of February. This time is set aside to honor African Americans whose contributions have had a significant impact on our country. This afternoon, it is our great pleasure to share with you one of the most important of these contributions–the African-American Spiritual.

Sing: "Ev'ry Time I Feel the Spirit"

Narrator 2:
During the 18th and 19th centuries, slaves had been brought from Africa to work in a new land, called America. They were forced to do hard labor. They built houses, cleared fields, planted and harvested crops like cotton, corn and tobacco. In addition to field work, they took care of the animals, cleaned the houses of their owners and cooked their food. They even helped raise the slave master's children.

They worked tirelessly from sun up to sun down, with little or no reward for their labor.

Sing: "Nobody Knows the Trouble I've Seen"

Narrator 1:
These African slaves, who had been captured and brought to America, had nothing. They had no shoes or earthly possessions of any kind. Their names were even changed. However, they did carry within their hearts, minds and souls, memories of their past life; their love for one another, their stories, their rhythms and their music. These were things that the slave master could not take away.

Sing: "Swing Low, Sweet Chariot"

Narrator 2:
The spiritual song grew out of the slaves' sadness and strong desire to go back to Africa. The songs helped to relieve their burdens. As they gathered to sing these songs, they felt hopeful that one day they would all be returned to their homeland.

Sing: "My Lord, What a Morning"

Narrator 1:
Slaves did not always feel sad. They had happy moments. They looked forward to a time when they could wear new shoes and have new clothes. They never lost hope that they would one day be free. "I've Got Shoes" is a spiritual that tells of these happy moments.

Sing: "I've Got Shoes"

Narrator 2:
Another happy spiritual is "Rock-a My Soul." This song represents the strong connection the slave had to the stories in the Old Testament of the Bible. Slaves believed that if God could help Little David overpower the Giant Goliath, Jonah survive being swallowed by a whale, and Moses lead tens of thousands of people across the Red Sea to freedom, he would also guide them out of slavery. It overjoyed the slave to hear these stories, so they made up songs about these biblical characters.

Sing: "Rock-a My Soul"

Narrator 2:
Slaves imagined an end to their pain and suffering. They imagined being free. They often sang about their freedom but they had to make their slave owners think they were singing about something else. To trick the slave master, they made up songs that contained codes. For example, in the spiritual "Go Down, Moses," the name ***Moses*** refers to Harriet Tubman who was a conductor of the Underground Railroad. She helped many slaves find their way to the North and to freedom. Her people nicknamed her Moses. ***Egypt land*** refers to the south where people were in slavery, and ***Pharaoh*** refers to the Master or overseer of the plantation. The ***people*** are the slaves. Harriet Tubman used this spiritual, "Go Down, Moses" as a signal to help slaves escape. As you listen to it, you should have a new understanding of what the lyrics or words are truly saying.

Sing: "Go Down, Moses"

Narrator 1:
When escaped slaves had reached safety in the North, songs would spread throughout the slave community to let everyone know all was well.

Sing: "Free at Last"

Narrator 2:
As we prepare to sing our final selection, we hope that you will take the message of our spiritual song with you. We ask you to join with us as we sing our final selection, "This Little Light of Mine."

Sing: "This Little Light of Mine"